# JOY
## ·TO THE·
# WORLD

*Favorite Carols From Many Lands*

## ORGAN ARRANGEMENTS
## BY JACK W. JONES

## CONTENTS

# Shawnee Press

EXCLUSIVELY DISTRIBUTED BY

HAL·LEONARD®
CORPORATION
7777 W. BLUEMOUND RD. P.O. BOX 13819 MILWAUKEE, WI 53213

Visit Shawnee Press Online at
www.shawneepress.com

# CONTENTS
(Alphabetical)

# VARIATIONS ON "JOY TO THE WORLD!"

Sw. Full to Gt. 8'
Gt. Full
Ped. Full

*Tune:* **ANTIOCH**
GEORGE FRIDERIC HANDEL (1685-1759)
*Arranged by* JACK W. JONES

I.

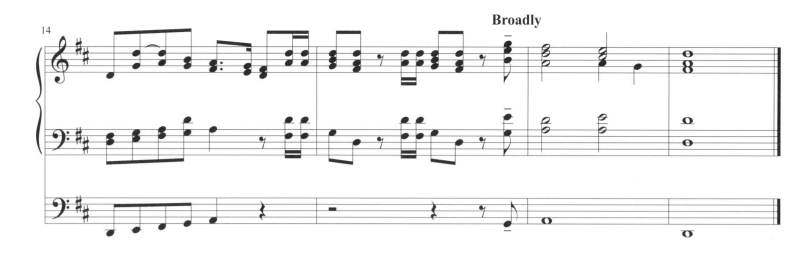

## II.

Pos. or Ch. 8', Fl. 8', 2'

**Articulate and light** ($\quarternote$ = 96)

*mf*

Manuals

VARIATIONS ON "JOY TO THE WORLD!"

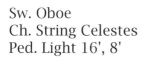
Sw. Oboe
Ch. String Celestes
Ped. Light 16', 8'

III.

**Grave** (♩ = 120)

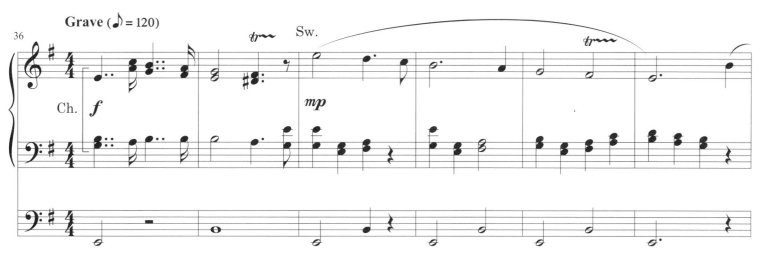

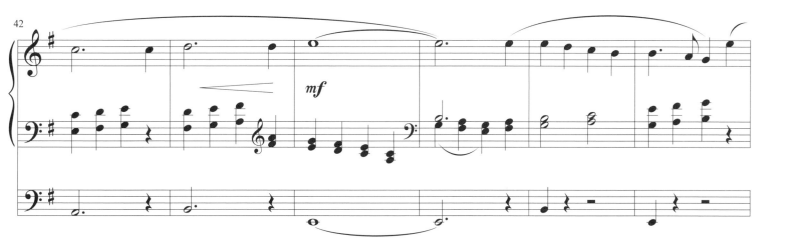

6

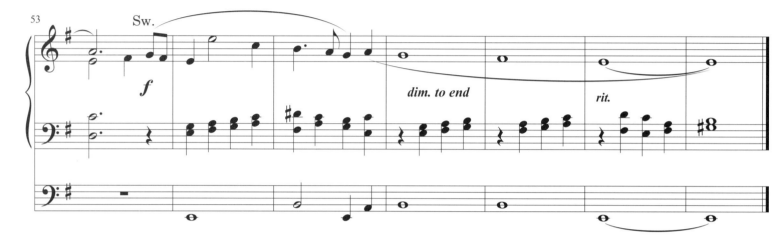

IV.

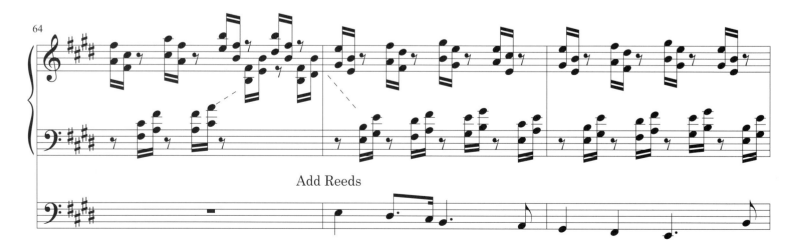

VARIATIONS ON "JOY TO THE WORLD!"

VARIATIONS ON "JOY TO THE WORLD!"

# RISE UP, SHEPHERD, AND FOLLOW

Gt. Solo
Ch. Flutes 8', 4'
Ped. 16' and 8'

Traditional Spiritual
*Arranged by* JACK W. JONES

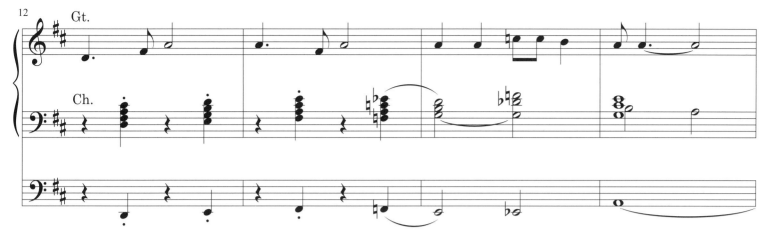

RISE UP, SHEPHERD, AND FOLLOW

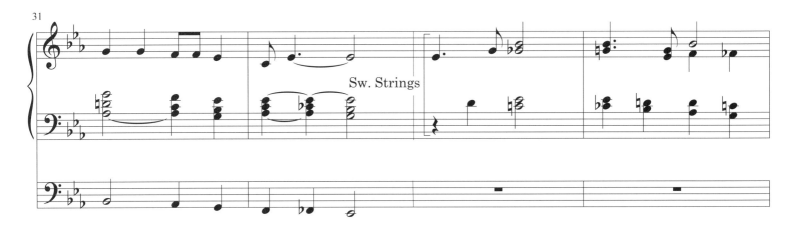

RISE UP, SHEPHERD, AND FOLLOW

# GOOD PEOPLE ALL, THIS CHRISTMAS TIME

Sw. Strings, Fl. 8'
Ch. Solo Reed or Flute
Ped. Soft 16', 8', Sw. to Pd.

*Tune:* **WEXFORD CAROL**
Irish Carol
*Arranged by* JACK W. JONES

GOOD PEOPLE ALL, THIS CHRISTMAS TIME

GOOD PEOPLE ALL, THIS CHRISTMAS TIME

# GOOD CHRISTIAN FRIENDS, REJOICE

Sw. Trumpet
Ch. Flutes 8', 2'
Ped. Light 16', 8', 4'

Tune: **IN DULCI JUBILO**
*Arranged by* JACK W. JONES

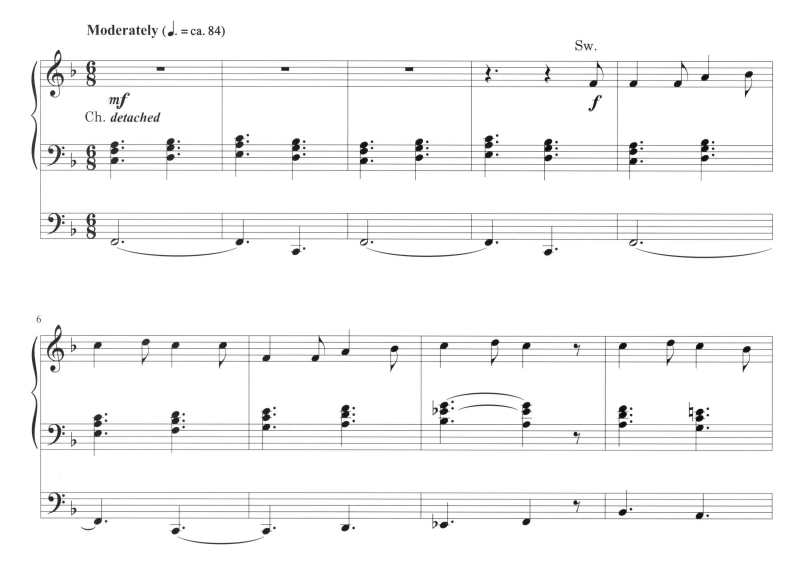

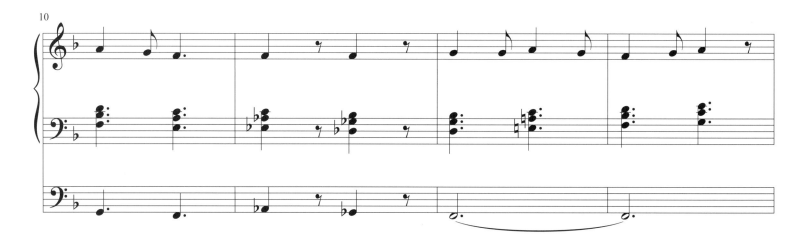

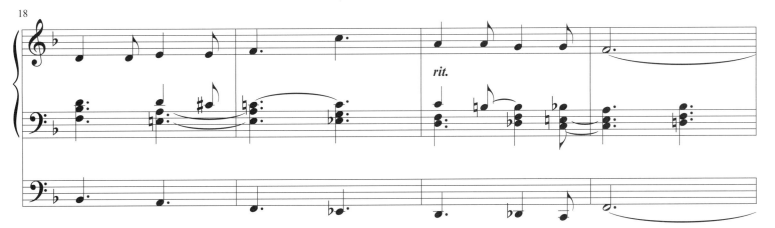

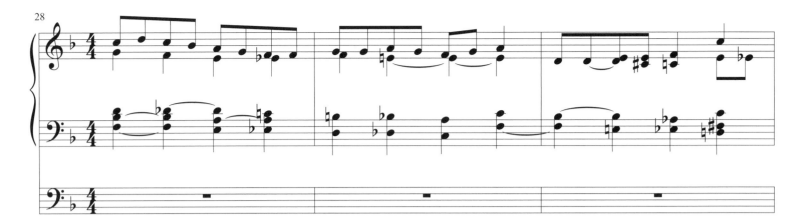

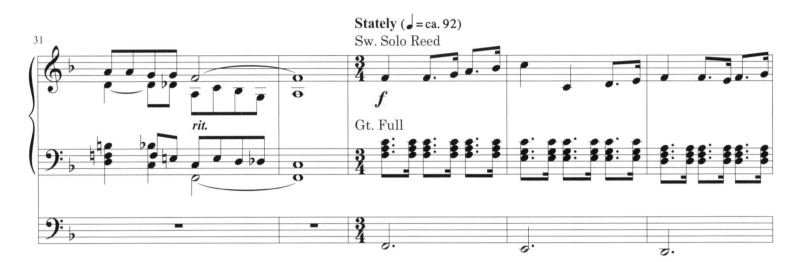

GOOD CHRISTIAN FRIENDS, REJOICE

GOOD CHRISTIAN FRIENDS, REJOICE

# ANGELS WE HAVE HEARD ON HIGH

Sw. Solo Trumpet
Gt.  Principals
Ped. Full 16', 8', 4'

*Tune:* **GLORIA**
Traditional French Melody
JACK W. JONES

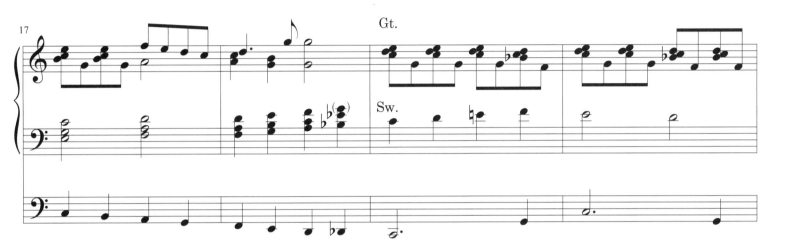

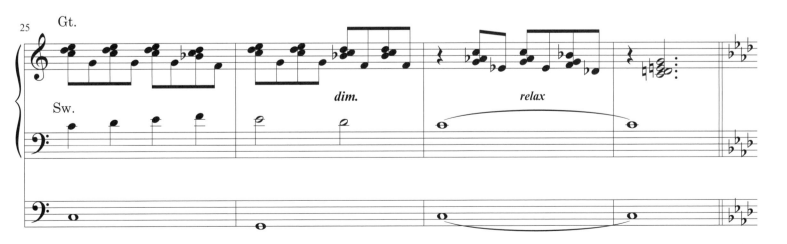

ANGELS WE HAVE HEARD ON HIGH

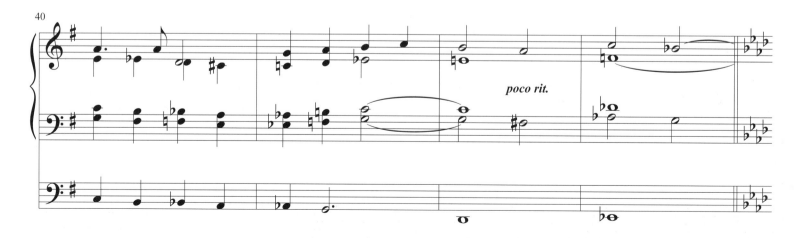

ANGELS WE HAVE HEARD ON HIGH

ANGELS WE HAVE HEARD ON HIGH

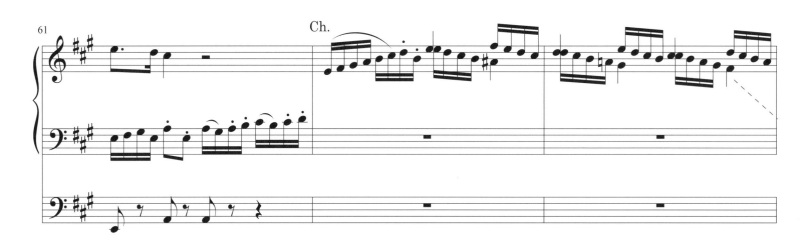

ANGELS WE HAVE HEARD ON HIGH

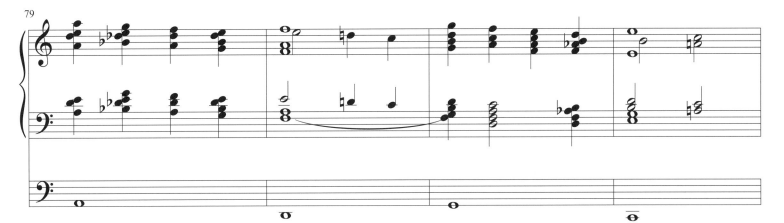

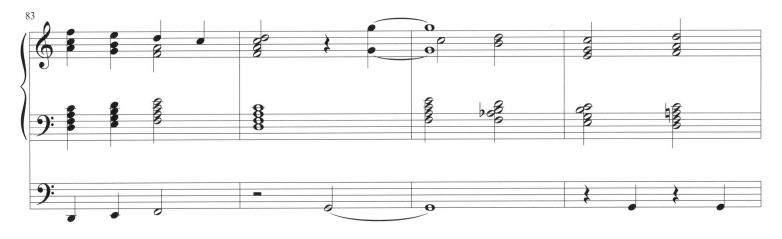

ANGELS WE HAVE HEARD ON HIGH

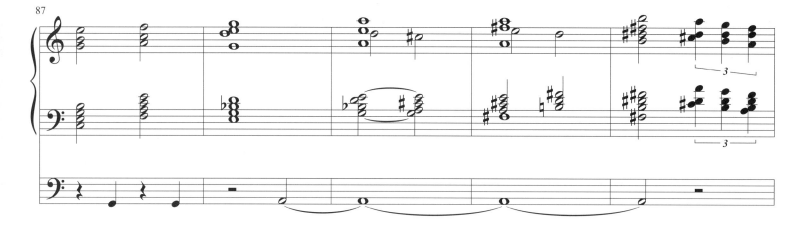

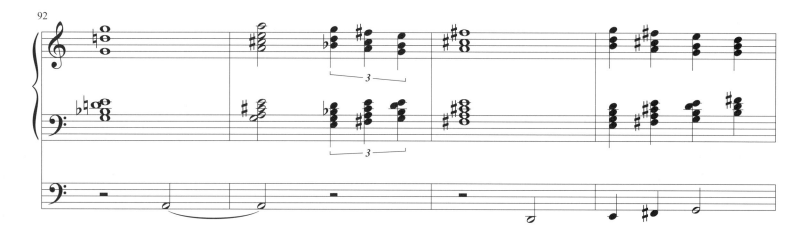

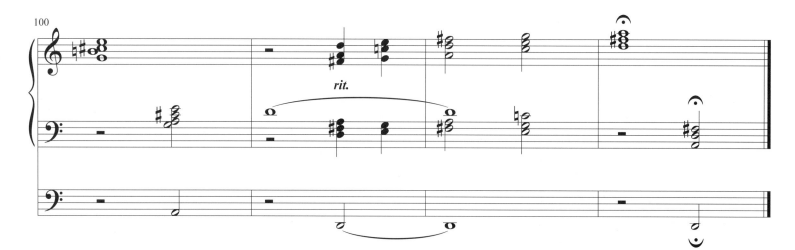

ANGELS WE HAVE HEARD ON HIGH

# INFANT HOLY, INFANT LOWLY

Sw. Strings, Flute 8'
Ch. Clarinet
Ped. Light 16', 8'

*Tune:* **W ZLOBIE LEZY**
Polish Folk Tune
*Arranged by* JACK W. JONES

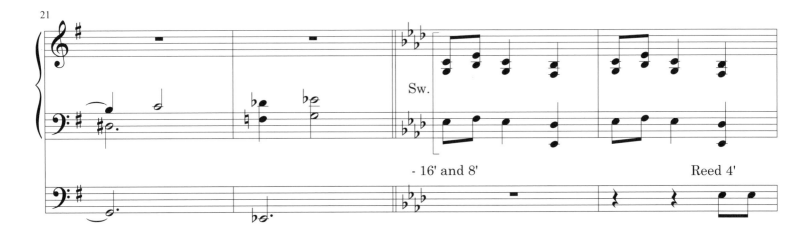

INFANT HOLY, INFANT LOWLY

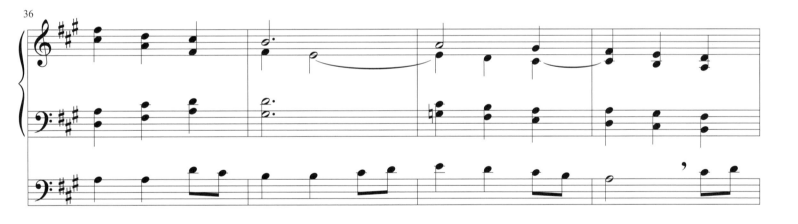

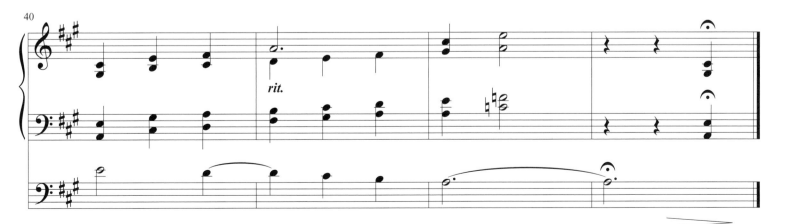

INFANT HOLY, INFANT LOWLY

# DING DONG! MERRILY ON HIGH

Sw. Trumpet
Ch. Flutes 8', 2'
Ped. Light 16', 8', 4'

French Melody, 16th c.
*Arranged by* JACK W. JONES

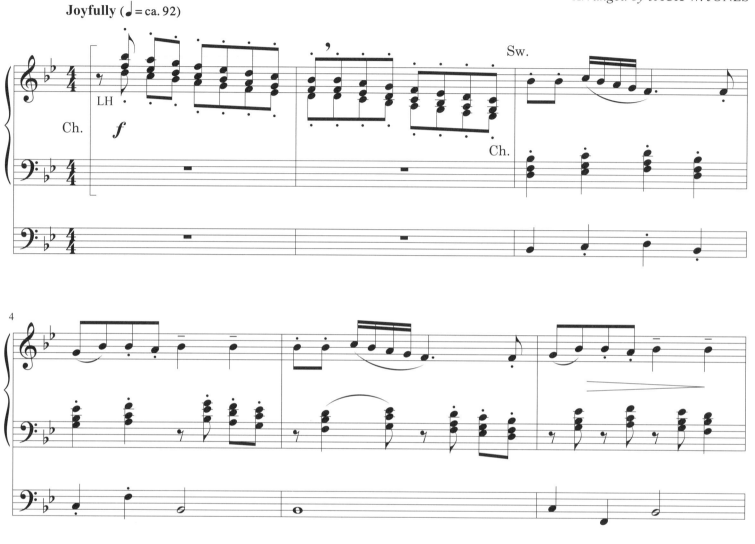

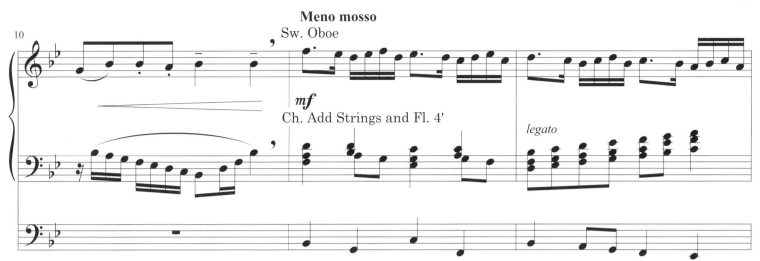

DING DONG! MERRILY ON HIGH

**Slow and majestic**

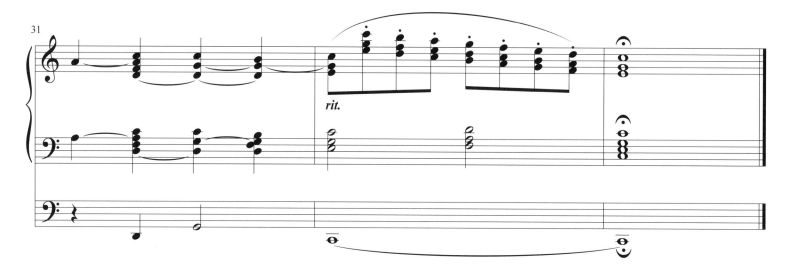

DING DONG! MERRILY ON HIGH

# COVENTRY CAROL

Sw. Strings
Ch. Clarinet
Ped. Soft 16', 8'

English Carol, 15th c.
*Arranged by* JACK W. JONES

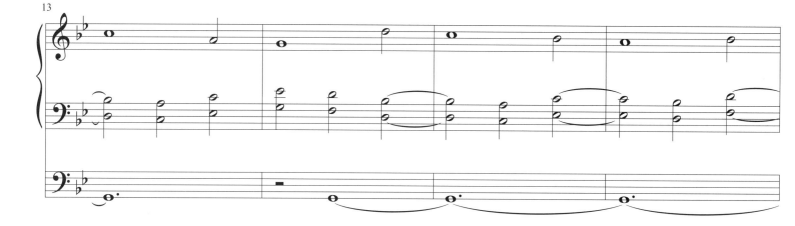

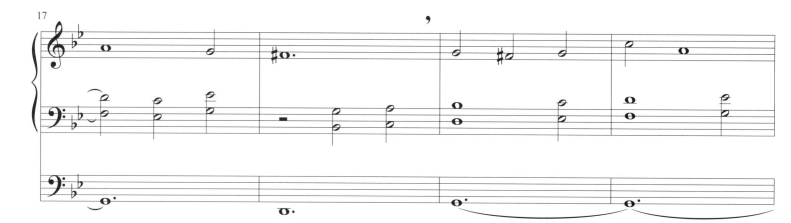

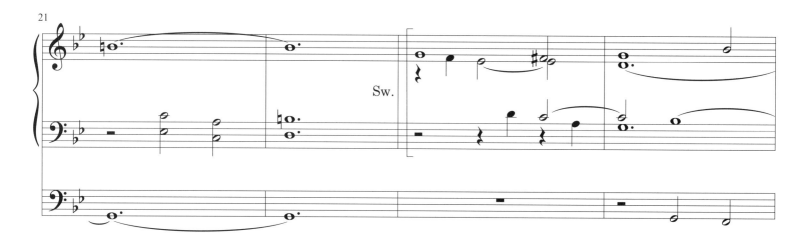

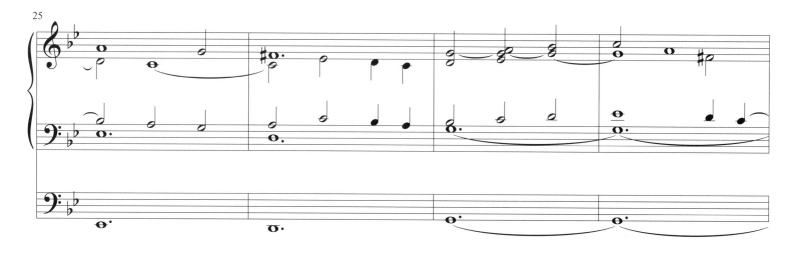

COVENTRY CAROL

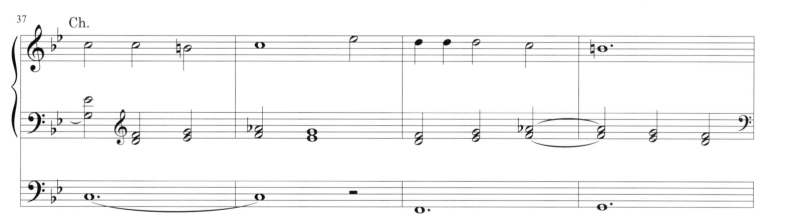

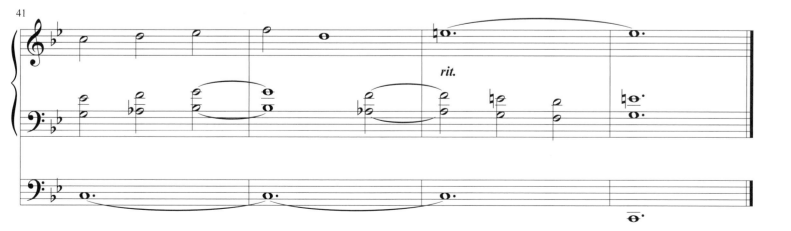

COVENTRY CAROL

# DECK THE HALL

Sw. Solo Trumpet
Gt. Full
Ch. Flutes 8', 2'
Ped. Full

Traditional Welsh Carol
*Arranged by* JACK W. JONES

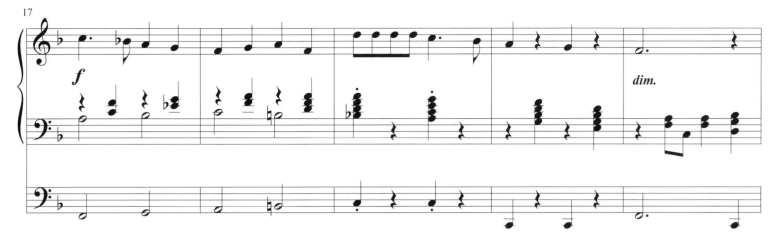

**Jubilantly** (♩ = ca. 112)

DECK THE HALL

DECK THE HALL

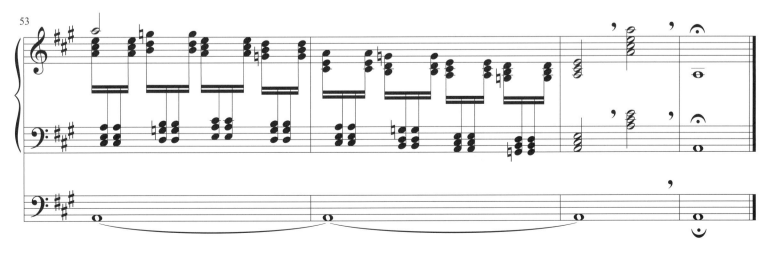

DECK THE HALL

# BEST-SELLING KEYBOARD COLLECTIONS

## from Shawnee Press

### CHRISTMAS EVERGREENS

*Shawnee Press*

Some of the greatest names in sacred piano music are celebrated in this Shawnee Select compendium making this the "must-have" keyboard collection of classic Christmas carols. Includes: Angels We Have Heard on High • What Child Is This? • Come Thou Long-Expected Jesus • The Friendly Beasts • Of the Father's Love Begotten • and more.

35003713  Piano Solo..............................$18.95

### EVENSONG

*Shawnee Press*

An outstanding compilation of songs of hope and reflection. Includes: Going Home • Tis So Sweet to Trust in Jesus • Improvisation on Balm in Gilead • I Am His and He is Mine • His Eye Is On the Sparrow • Fairest Lord Jesus • All Through the Night • My Jesus, I Love Thee • Nearer, Still Nearer • and more.

35006102  Piano Solo..............................$18.95

### GO OUT IN JOY – FESTIVE POSTLUDES FOR PIANO

*Harold Flammer Music*

Finally a piano collection that provides the perfect selection for jubilant postludes and festive encores! A variety of styles and difficulty levels are included, with careful attention paid to choose hymns that have the spirit of celebration in both tune and text. Enjoy the work of Vicki Tucker Courtney, Cindy Berry, Brad Nix, Alex-Zsolt, Hojun Lee and others!

35028092  Piano Solo..............................$16.99

### GOSPEL GOLD

*Featuring Arrangements from: Cindy Berry, Patti Drennan, Mark Hayes, Lloyd Larson, and others*
*Shawnee Press*

Some of today's best pianists and arrangers have gathered to celebrate the best timeless gospel hymns in a new compilation sure to be a hit with any church pianist. 17 songs, including: Stand Up, Stand Up for Jesus • 'Tis So Sweet to Trust in Jesus • Just a Closer Walk with Thee • Do Lord • Rock of Ages • He Keeps Me Singing • and many more.

35027306  Piano Solo..............................$14.95

### GOSPEL GOLD – VOLUME 2

*GlorySound*

Energized by the success of *Gospel Gold,* enjoy this celebrated sequel perfect for every occasion. Like its predecessor, this compilation is essential repertoire for every church pianist. Fifteen favorite hymns and gospel tunes leap from the pages in these exciting new arrangements. Sizzling southern gospel, ragtime, and even jazz treatments infuse this collection with variety and joy.

35028093  Piano Solo..............................$16.99

### HOLY, HOLY, HOLY

*Shawnee Press*

9 songs arranged for piano and organ duet, including: Fairest Lord Jesus • Holy Holy Holy • In the Garden • O Sacred Head, Now Wounded • and more. 2 books provided, one for each player.

35009567  Piano/Organ Duets................$39.99

### THE HOLLY AND THE IVORY

*Featuring arrangements from Heather Sorenson, Lee Dengler, Matt Hyzer, Shirley Brendlinger, Brad Nix, and others*
*Shawnee Press*

A Christmas gift for every church pianist, this new compilation is filled with wonderful carol arrangements for sanctuary or concert use. Includes: The Holly and the Ivy • Bring a Torch, Jeanette Isabella • Once in Royal David's City • The Huron Carol • and many others.

35027913  Piano Solo..............................$16.95

### HYMNS OF GRATEFUL PRAISE

*arr. Lee Dengler*
*Shawnee Press*

These artful arrangements are a pianist's dream – filling the air with a variety of beautiful moments, well designed to the hand and heart of the performer. Includes: For the Beauty of the Earth • Morning Has Broken • Fairest Lord Jesus • Now Thank We All Our God • Holy God We Praise Thy Name • All Creatures of Our God and King • Praise Him! Praise Him! • and more.

35028339  Piano Solo..............................$16.99

### IMAGES

*arr. Heather Sorenson*
*Shawnee Press*

These highly impressionistic arrangements are designed to capture the ear and eye while portraying the spirit of each of the arrangements. When combined with the innovative visual supplement, the church pianist moves their ministry from its traditional role into a new area of expression. Includes: Beautiful • I Surrender All • Fairest Lord Jesus • I Must Tell Jesus • It Is Well • Whiter Than Snow • A Mighty Fortress • and more.

35028265  Piano Book.........................$16.99

### JOY TO THE WORLD
*arr. Jack Jones*
*Shawnee Press*
Take a holiday trip around the world with this exceptional collection of carols. This cadre of favorites offers variety of style and idiom that add color to your seasonal programming. Includes: Joy to the World • Angels We Have Heard on High • Coventry Carol • Deck the Hall • Ding Dong! Merrily on High! • Good Christians, All Rejoice • Good People All This Christmas Time • Infant Holy, Infant Lowly • Rise Up, Shepherd, and Follow.
35028373  Organ Solo.............................$16.99

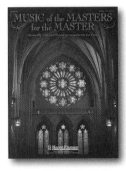

### MUSIC OF THE MASTERS FOR THE MASTER
*Harold Flammer Music*
This unique collection for the church pianist displays the arranging skills of some of today's best keyboard writers. Using a classical theme or genre as the basis for each piece, the composer weds a time-honored hymn to bring these beloved themes into the sanctuary. Included in this thoughtful assembly is the writing of Mary McDonald, Cindy Berry, Carolyn Hamlin, Joseph Martin, Alex-Zsolt, Jack Jones, James Michael Stevens and many others.
35028091  Piano Solo.............................$19.99

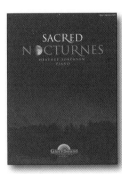

### SACRED NOCTURNES
*by Heather Sorenson*
*Shawnee Press*
Beautiful arrangements for offertories, communion, and other special events. Includes: I Will Arise and Go to Jesus • Be Thou My Vision • This Is My Father's World • At Day's End • Shall We Gather at the River • A Reflection on the Cross • All Through the Night • Be Still My Soul • Nearer, My God, to Thee • Turn Your Eyes Upon Jesus • 'Til We Meet Again.
35018775  Piano Solo.............................$18.95

### SANCTUARY
*arr. Ruth Schram*
*Shawnee Press*
A fine collection of sacred, well-crafted piano arrangements. Includes: O How I Love Jesus • Jesus Paid It All • The Solid Rock • Go Tell It on the Mountain • Onward Christian Soldiers • Be Thou My Vision.

35018856  Piano Solo.............................$14.95

### SANCTUARY SKETCHES
*arr. Matt Hyzer*
*GlorySound*
These short, yet musically complete, arrangements can be used in a variety of worship settings and the assortment of styles employed makes them a fresh approach to service playing needs. Contents: Alleluia! Sing to Jesus • Christ Arose • Crown Him with Many Crowns • Go, Tell It on the Mountain • Amazing Grace • It Is Well with My Soul • Do Lord • Jesus Loves Me • and more.
35018861  Piano Solo.............................$9.95

### SIMPLY BEAUTIFUL
*Shawnee Press*
Mary McDonald, Heather Sorenson, Cindy Berry, Dan Forrest, Joel Raney, Joseph Martin and many others combine to make this an essential collection for your sacred keyboard needs. Includes: Be Thou My Vision • I Am Bound for the Promised Land • I Am His and He Is Mine • Tis So Sweet to Trust In Jesus • What a Friend We Have in Jesus • and many more.
35027735  Piano Solo.............................$16.95

### SNOW FALLING ON IVORY – VOLUME 1
*Featuring arrangements by Joseph M. Martin, Lloyd Larson, Mark Hayes, Heather Sorenson & more*
*GlorySound*
Pianists may play the arrangements as piano solos or perform them in tandem with the optional instrumental descants for something truly special. Includes: Away in a Manger • Dance at the Manger • Ding Dong Merrily on High • Gesu Bambino • Go, Tell It on the Mountain • He Shall Feed this Flock with "My Shepherd Will Supply My Need" • In the Bleak Mid-Winter • Infant Holy with "He Is Born" • It Came Upon a Midnight Clear • Let All Mortal Flesh Keep Silence • Three Carols of Comfort and Joy • Wexford Carol.
35020710  Piano Solo.............................$24.95

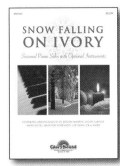

### SNOW FALLING ON IVORY – VOLUME 2
*GlorySound*
Like the inaugural book in this series, this volume of beloved Christmas carols is a two-in-one sensation. Pianists may play the arrangements as piano solos or perform them in tandem with the optional instrumental descants for something truly special. This unique format doubles your performance options and makes this compilation an excellent value. From tender carols of reflection to sparkling songs of joy, these books are a one-stop resource for holiday service playing. Arrangers include: Joseph Martin, John Purifoy, Lee Dengler, Vicki Tucker Courtney, Brad Nix, Harry Strack, Matt Hyzer, Shirley Brendlinger, Alex-Zsolt, James Koerts and Joel Raney.
35028386  Piano Solo.............................$19.99

### TWO VOICES ONE SONG
*arr. Carolyn Hamlin*
*Harold Flammer Music*
Carolyn Hamlin tastefully handles the interaction of piano and organ giving each a chance to shine during the arrangements. Includes: Rejoice, the Lord is King • O Love of God, Most Full • All Cratures of Our God and King • Joy to the World • Softly and Tenderly • God and Grace and God of Glory • Go So Loved the World • God Save Our Native Land • Jesus Shall Reign.
35024487  Piano/Organ Duets.............................$16.95

## Shawnee Press

EXCLUSIVELY DISTRIBUTED BY

**HAL•LEONARD®**
CORPORATION
7777 W. BLUEMOUND RD. P.O. BOX 13819 MILWAUKEE, WI 53213